DINOSAURS
COLORING BOOK

JAN SOVAK

D1432931

DOVER PUBLICATIONS, INC.
MINEOLA, NEW YORK

Copyright

Copyright © 2014 by Dover Publications, Inc.
All rights reserved.

Bibliographical Note

Dinosaurs Coloring Book, first published by Dover Publications, Inc., in 2014, is a compilation of *Dinosaurs! Coloring Book* and *Dinosaurs of the Jurassic Era,* both published by Dover in 2009.

International Standard Book Number

ISBN-13: 978-0-486-77960-7
ISBN-10: 0-486-77960-2

Manufactured in the United States by Courier Corporation
77960203   2014
www.doverpublications.com

NOTE

Millions of years ago, the earth was very different than it is today. There were no people, and reptiles called dinosaurs inhabited the earth. There were many different kinds of dinosaurs. Some were huge, and could grow up to fifty feet tall, some were small, some walked on two legs, some walked on four, some were speedy, and some were slow. Some ate meat, and others ate plants. Some had armor-plated skin, and some had horns. Then, 65 million years ago, the dinosaurs suddenly became extinct. All that remains of the dinosaurs today are fossils. No one knows exactly what noises the dinosaurs made, what color they were, how their skin felt, or how they behaved, but after spending many years studying the fossils of these impressive reptiles, scientists now understand more about their amazing prehistoric world. So just add color to artist Jan Sovak's beautiful illustrations to experience for yourself the life of the dinosaurs!

Augustinia

Allosaurus

Amargasaurus

Apatosaurus

Carnotaurus

Cryolophosaurus

Diplodocus

Euoplocephalus

Gastonia

Giganotosaurus

Hypsilophodon

Iguanodon

Maiasaura

Mamenchisaurus

Mononykus

Oviraptor

Pachyrhinosaurus

Parasaurolophus

Scipionyx

Spinosaurus

Stegosaurus

Struthiomimus

Stygimoloch

Styracosaurus

Suchomimus

Triceratops

Troodon

Tyrannosaurus Rex

Utahraptor

Velociraptor

Allosaurus

Apatosaurus

Camarasaurus

Camptosaurus

Ceratosaurus

Compsognathus

Cryolophosaurus

Dilophosaurus

Diplodocus

Edmarka

Fabrosaurus

Gasosaurus

Heterodontosaurus

Huayangosaurus

Kentrosaurus

Koparion

Lufengosaurus

Mamenchisaurus

Megalosaurus

Metriacanthosaurus

Monolophosaurus

Ornitholestes

Othnielia

Piatnitzkysaurus

Sauroposeidon

Shunosaurus

Sinraptor

Supersaurus

Tuojiangosaurus

Yangchuanosaurus